Constant Longing

Also by Dennis Sampson

The Double Genesis
Forgiveness

Dennis Sampson

Constant Longing

poems

Carnegie Mellon University Press
Pittsburgh 2000

Acknowledgments

Some of these poems first appeared—at times in different versions—in the following magazines: *The American Voice*, *The Ohio Review*, and *Shenandoah*. "The Anaconda" received a Pushcart Prize in 1995.

Publication of this book is supported by a grant from the Pennsylvania Council on the Arts.

Contents

for Louie Skipper

The sun, with planets revolving around it and depending on it, still shines on a bunch of grapes as if there were nothing else in the universe to do.

—Galileo

ONE

Evening Inventory

I wanted to praise the moral quality
of the black ant, the ministry of the heron,
the dove that built a nest above my door-sill,
the potato for being so blunt, the bread,
the brown field, the bashful Blue Columbine;
my careful account of all I had seen that was needed.

How easily the worn soul comes now to peace
with the appearance of the apostle of a tree.
Its logic is of the dawn
and of the evening. Let me endure
in my grandeur, in my dark poverty, in my wild ways.
With all that follows. With all that flows and sways.

And I am in love again with the light
on stone columns of the cathedral
riding the silence of the mind, with sympathy
for the fist clenched against winter: Larkspur,
thistle, slate and quartz—Yellow Sand Verbena.
Names. And situations. And the strong heart that stays.

The firmament falls back; the constellations
slide. Sleep comes to the Wild Gourd,
the Globe Lily, the hawk in silhouette.
The ecumenical council of the crows has ceased.
And another spirit that does not speak
sees everything: Primose, Mariposa, Golden Pea.

Speaking The Names

When you found the nest of a hummingbird
   below the pond,
                you told me you had looked
     for years,
and I wondered where the ruby-throated
                hummingbird

had gone,
       a flash flowing back to this sanctuary
of threaded vine. The past
   yields up a dozen or so
such images, you surprised by the appearance

       of a hummingbird in June
and the Japanese maple that asked for hope
and charity
on your patio. Do you remember not knowing the
              names of trees?

   How could you tell a hickory from an ash?
   How could you tell a sycamore from a poplar?

   Bending the branch
that gripped the palm-sized nest, it snapped,
       and later I squeezed that stem
in a chink by my study window,
     where it recalls our walk in early March.

      Facing the figure of Magdalene
that day, I thought I saw not one

but many hummingbirds,
and I have searched for other nests
since then, and, in my haste, found nothing,

yet I know the names of trees
and say their names: dogwood, water-oak, and pine.

Coming Back To Keats

In the night that is quiet, where I can't see,
in a stand of trees, a single bird begins.
    What he sings for, loud and clear, as if he had
                too much

to say to get into the day, to whom he sings,
remains a mystery. Wait for this blessing
    throughout the neighborhood to fade,

    heart-felt, uttered without complaint to the moon
or maybe to himself, as in another song by Keats
             who listened
    to the nightingale and tried to cling

    to its delicious reverie. Feel pain
as he goes on to speak of things
    not seen (as he's not seen) on a night when
             nobody

    steps outside in awe of starlight across the sky.
What bird is this? An oriole out late?
    The elusive soloist has nothing and everything

to say, withdrawing his invitation to savor
             what remains
after the cardinals have flown, and the jays.
    Then very gently silence begins again

      as if it had never been away, three notes, staccato,
coming near, stumbling on something more—not in
             the least afraid.
    Lulled by this improvisational trill,

  this silence in which everything is known,
           nothing revealed,
I can't help relishing what I know will cease
  when I have closed the front door, darkened
             the hall,

  drifted off to sleep in the middle of the night
with the light of the clock on my face,
  only to rise an hour later, wild-eyed, afraid.

Impossible to sleep. Impossible to stay awake.

The Good Night Of Sleep

Light rain in the trees. The ghost
in your dreams. The gift of imagining.
The gift of seeing. The wren at morning
followed out of sight along with its mate.

Nightwatch. The need for sleep.
Slide and release. Someone you can't reach
in the long dark. The scream. Evening
neither at peace with you nor you with evening.

The shape that appears in the entranceway.
Even unbelief. Knuckle-bone and ring.
Even what you can't think.
The heart, so far obedient, fleeing.

The Snapping Turtle At Templeton Pond

My friend once reeled something in
from far off, pulled up from the floor of a pond
when he was a kid, neither swerving from one side
to the other (but clearly alive) nor fighting back,
a great weight that finally showed itself under
the surface as a shape darker than water with glints
of yellow. "It burst up," he said, "its forefeet braced
on concrete, as if it wanted to see what had done this,
then snapped the line." My friend's eyes widened

but I was lost in the descent,
a ribbon of blood trailing from my jaw
until at last I settled along the bottom.
A cloud of silt rises up, fish flick away
as if of one mind, a wreath of weed waving
from around my neck. Then memory fails me
after an hour of stillness and circumspection
from the depths, and I am left to dwell
on a disturbance of the heart—the knowledge
of what sought me out of all the turtles in the world
vanishing.

And then, of course,
everything forgets me—and is forgotten.
I work free the hook, scraped along the flesh
of my palate, it sways off, borne upward
by the nylon line.

If you see me
in your sleep and feel the fear of death
because you understand, if you think
me a deity that willingly drew close,

certain at first I came against my will,
picked me up, peered into my eyes,
felt the need to prepare for the inevitable
you got wrong, gazing up like a brutal patriarch
awakened by laughter in the middle of the night,
remember: I am what I am and have
no choice. If you want me to be a god
you should have told me
and I would have dragged you down into the dark.

In Hell

What a tremendous height you have come down from,
       with filthy wings,
              picking through offal
      scooped and flung at your feet,
  your retinue of demons
          driven from the excrement
on which you perpetually feast.

       What a tremendous height,
  and what grief
for the ones who have come to resemble you
      completely,
           relishing the shriek,
    the hunt through slime
—oblivious of the orgy that suddenly ceases

  without the slightest hint
of release—begins again,
     while you sit up and see
  what you have wrought
from your ridiculous promontory in the heat,
      drawing your sleeve across your mouth,
dreaming of other Edens.

     I have seen you leaning
in my mind's eye, your thick face pitted and swollen
      from lack of sleep,
   gesturing with fingers elegant
    and flecked with blood,
unaware how apparent your hideousness is to me.

   Do you ever long for an hour of leisure

in the shade of a tree,
                drinking martinis,
        the young seductress linking her arm
      in yours
as if she were afraid you might leave?
                    In sunglasses? Scented with lotions?
      Satisfied for the moment to simply be?

   Do you remember what it was to feel
heaven on your face,
            taking your meaning from The Meaning
as long as you conceded you were one
      among many,
                and being one, were all
looking up in unison at what you believed?

What a tremendous height you have come down from,
utterly defeated,
        preening as if to be rid of the shit
on your wings, issuing decrees,
                turning ever so slowly to meet my eyes
        this evening—keeping after me—
as if something unknown made obedience necessary.

Laundry In Venice

—for Fran Levine

Your painting Laundry in Venice came today
and I have to tell you I was shocked

at just how beautiful it was,
so finely done I studied each subtle brush-stroke

before putting it up on the wall of my study. Of course
it brought back memories of you showing me slides

last August outside the laundromat in Vermont,
too modest to accept my praise for your accomplishment.

In your letter you inquire about my writing.
Last December I was there for the death

of a friend and unsuccessfully tried
to write her into a poem that went nowhere.

I wasn't sure what anyone could say of a life
lived so much off to the side, remembering

the photograph I saw of Stephanie at eleven
in the camera's eye with her cheerleading

outfit on and finding it almost impossible to fathom
God would have the audacity to set before

this girl the dying she would endure
for seven years. She seemed so thin,

looking shyly out over the passage of time,
to ever be touched by such pain.

But touched she was. Those of us who loved her
let her go because we had no other choice,

having watched her struggle to stay alive
so many years. Once, when she was in Texas,

she sent me a postcard of the hospital,
M.D. Anderson, which simply said on the back

"Dear Dennis, having a wonderful time,
wish you were here." And I thought if someone

having a bone-marrow transplant could still retain
her lightness there was hope, not only for her, but for
                                                            us all.

She fought so hard, with fierceness,
through chemotherapy that turned her skeletal,

heroic, an outcast with an outrageous wig
that struggled to conceal what she was going through,

fought against the notion of her mortality
and the conclusion that she would have to come to

that everything she held most dear
would be left behind. I delighted in making her laugh

till she was in tears, in the pleasure she took
in showing me around her garden before she died,

pointing out each flower, calla lilies and
                              chrysanthemums,
the time we danced together at Ed's wedding.

How beautiful she looked in her new swimming suit
the summer her husband and I broiled miserably

in the heat at Lake Nichol. I wished, but for her,
we were sitting before an air-conditioner, drinking
                              cold beer.

Foolish to imagine what wisdom she must be blessed with
certain she will be waiting for me when my time
                              has arrived.

Do you remember our walk to the house we thought
was Robert Frost's? That woman

with her back to us as we came up
haunts me still. From behind she looked exactly

as I imagined Frost—short and squat,
with a shock of silver hair. And I remember

how cordial she was, not getting up
from her chair and strangely letting us walk

around her house: you, me, Tracy,
Andrea and Jill. Didn't we even go in?

When did we realize this wasn't
Frost's house at all, that she was merely staying here

and that Frost's house was further on?
Was that after we left or did she inform us

of our error while we were there?
And I remember asking you about the life

of the first poet I read and loved so many years ago,
James Wright, when I was in my twenties,

and you told the story about his visit to Fresno,
the glass of vodka filled to the top at breakfast

because Phil made the mistake of saying
"Just say When," the poet as tender in his poetry

as one can get without going mad, and bitter too
because what he cherished in this world was

being defiled, the kind of poet I idealized once
and tried to mimic but that I consider

differently now remembering he was human
and doing what he could to simply survive.

I first read his poetry when I was a roofer
in South Dakota, over twenty years ago,

and I still have what looks like a rash
across my knee, having clumsily allowed

that hellish fluid of hot tar to find its way
through a slit, affixing itself to my skin.

And I remember, too, one weekend took us to a city
where we spent three nights up the street

from the theater whose roof we had to strip,
peeling back that ancient layer in the heat

before preparations for the new roof could begin.
Beyond the trees lay the glittering Missouri,

ultramarine in the distance, and while I resolved
to throw myself in at the end of every day,

after I had taken a shower and had a few beers
it never ever occurred to me again.

I looked at that river with the same craving
I did those thunderheads that murmured

on the horizon then turned left over the plains,
God's fault, whom I rebuked in silence in my heart.

And it was strange being awakened in the dark
by another man, the fist at the door

followed by "Dennis, get up!" and I would lie
and listen to the fist all down the hallway

then put my feet on the floor. Next to my bed lay
The Branch Will Not Break. And I would pick up

Wright's book and slide it inside my bag
 so the maid wouldn't think I was crazy, the prospect

of returning on a day humid and blazing, of climbing
that long precarious ladder which would lift

just a little as I stepped out onto the roof
even with the treetops, one I didn't relish in the least.

If the poet knew what I was doing in that room
he would have been appreciative, don't you think?

But what I am leading up to, Fran,
is that my last night there I discovered

coming up the stairs no matter how many books
you've read there is a bewildering flipside

to the good life I had lived, all whining
about an unjust world washed away by awe

when I walked out into the hallway lit
by one ceiling light and heard a voice

neither feminine nor male crying from one
of the rooms off to my left. Were they calling me?

No. They were beseeching nothing in this world,
not God, nor the nearness of loved ones;

not the hope of a life that would eventually get better
from the darkness I knew looked just like mine.

I felt pity for all women and men and was afraid
of opening that door to a figure reaching

out its hand to me and that, without saying anything,
would beg me to stay throughout the night.

Then crying ceased, although I waited long
for it to revive, inching back into the shadows

when one of the other men emerged from his room,
a towel wrapped round his waist. Next morning

I found that door wide open and the bed made,
every trace of their being there swept clean.

It would be twenty-five years before I understood
what inspired that cry and what it meant to me,

carrying Stephanie out to her father's van
the day she died, in her blue and yellow bathrobe.

Every now and then she would lift her hand
in the mirror and groan and I wanted to scream

when the lights turned red on me,
cutting recklessly in and out,

traffic emphasizing what Auden meant
about Icarus falling into the sea,

that life goes on no matter what
and the slightest hint of weakness

can be our destroyer even in a dark red van
veering north with a family perfectly aware

their daughter will not see the sun again,
her cry coming again despite what Stephanie's

mother said when I looked back at her,
that Stephanie didn't feel anything.

But our walk was a memorable one,
in the heat and shade of a gravel path

through the Vermont hillside,
then up the highway with pastures cast in soft light,

one I hope to repeat someday
if there is any justice. It is June,

and what I originally thought was a mockingbird
sings from the upper branches of a hickory

across the street so passionately
you'd think it knew of something that could not

be denied, like your desire to affirm for me
while looking up at laundry

a world beautiful and ordinary and true
with that Italian morning opening wide.

Variegated Arbicola: An Elegy

I wanted it to live awhile
along the window where the light
   required to survive is bright.

   But the leaves
turned golden after a month
   and lots of water failed

   to lift the spirit of this long
green silence tumbling over the rim
   of its pot. It got sick,

   a source of guilt
originally meant to show my single life
   was gifted in good measure

   with flourishings like this.
And nothing changed the way it felt
   although I moved it closer

   to the light, panicking at the thought
 something gently said
   might revive its pleasure in existence.

   Should I have done as others did,
my chair pulled close asking questions
   designed to get it to confess

   all it really wanted was attention?
But it was too obsessed
   to listen to the one who picked it out

and brought it home to be alone
with the desire for absolutely nothing else.
   Flop-eared monarch of a kingdom

   that didn't care, chronically depressed,
it got the best of me
   and I lugged it out of sight

   of the window in the yard
where it could wither all it wished,
   unsettled by this life that I'd

   been given to neglect.
I had thoughts of other plants,
   of bringing it back in,

   but after a week of worrying
forgot about it altogether.
   Bent down to retrieve a pen

   this morning, leaf crackling in my hand,
I remembered how,
   struggling to straighten the stems,

   it clambered up my neck and grazed my face
as if we both deserved respect
   for all the important words we never said.

What Is Written Down

Call it love gone wrong or something
just as deceptive and you find yourself fumbling again
in the light of the porch for the key
during that interim at twilight
when the neighborhood's empty
and the woman in pin-curlers stands
at the kitchen window washing dishes
as symbol of the life you could not live.

This is the witness turning back again
to the canticle of blossoms borne across the lawn
on an afternoon when no one comes through
the door to inquire why,
to inquire where,
written down in language in love with itself,
a conversation with the dead
that stops at the threshold of the century,
a monologue of jumbled praise that has
as its brother, solitude, its sister despair.

This is the testimony of the leaves
torn from the hickory in bleak November
revised and clarified
till only the mysterious truth reveals
what's left of a marriage
is not the issue, and never is.

Death is the issue, and what it does
to the chameleon that sees clearly
each petal relenting in the garden
behind a two-story house where someone
still frets over the lateness of the day, the season,

Stephanie preparing dinner in her bathrobe,
shadow among shadows, almost a shape,
shooing a moth through the window
with a hand that never looked so pale and thin.

And out of this revelation appears
a purposeful figure bereft of everything
that's cherished, a specter
come from some other place
to show you the way was not the way,
the path not a path, and all your preparations
a waste until you can explain
to yourself why you believed you even needed the key
now disengaged from its chain
to get you through the entrance no longer there.

Blue Photograph

—Alabama coast, spring 1995

If you were going in search of a single theme
that would redeem you, this driftwood
off the coast would be to your pleasing,
imprisoned within the lull and sway
of the sea, within the vertigo of ferocious water.

In a script like that of an animal's hieroglyphics
in the sand, nothing of what you witnessed
can be translated
where land and sea face each other in enmity.

Alone on the beach, in this blue photograph,
your eighty-two-year-old father stands in an open jacket
with his pants whipped back against his shins,
your mother sitting with a camera that won't flash
then does. When you told him

this was the photograph you loved above all the others
he was shocked. Time claws
at the mind,
and the three of you ground down by a multitude of suns
reject that archaic craving
erased as it is being realized toward whatever future is
                                        left to unlearn.

Devotional

Let's erect a tomb to someone stupid,
one antiquity can't match
nor the ancient civilizations of India and China.
Make it massive and immovable
against the earthquake's fury;
a monument to the accomplishments of yours truly.

There will be a citadel, like an upraised finger,
meant as a guide for the humorless
traveling by sea, the penitent, the devotee,
with rumors of instantaneous healings,
of demons wrenched from the ear
from gazing at this monstrosity to me.

It will persevere long after the millenniums,
long after the Mediterranean has turned to silt
and death can't be remembered
and time no longer whittles away at the skin,
a stupendous tomb, crafted by hands
too numerous to fathom, impervious, clean.

Let eternal longing possess my corpse completely,
my bones, my fingernails, my raving mane,
decked in emeralds, with all sorts of insignias,
a tomb scented with frankincense and myrrh,
and with a labyrinth that grieves
for the one who sought to save herself in me.

A Passion In The Desert

Oh they were in love all right. You could tell
by the way her eyes fixed on his while he was speaking
with the perseverance of a cheetah
that sees from its veil of grass the perfect gazelle,
this student of the cello come to meet my friend

in his forties, still bewildered by the death of his wife
whom I had known for nearly twenty years. And when
                                    he rose
to go she reached without thinking
as if to suppress a piece of sheet music lifted by wind,
and pulled on his sleeve, drawing him back and inquiring

where they might continue their discussion
on the cello. This was the beginning
and the end, passion that leaves one breathless,
sleepless nights with the smell of someone fresh
in your arms, ecstatic explanations of other loves

so unfulfilling: the pianist with a goatee, the
                            sullen mechanic
from Louisiana. I watched them reunite again and again
at his office, the furtive look
over the shoulder and opening of the door into which
                            she vanished
and thought how good that they had found each other.

Oh they were in love all right, this widower
and girl who admitted she once burst into tears
                            in Pittsburgh

because she had no idea how to find the exit
in a bookstore, with a father she was afraid to be alone with
returning nightly from this disastrous world to her nest
                                        for reassurance.

There was a kind of secrecy to everything,
long walks, rendezvous at the beach to see the sun
come up for them alone on the balcony, wrapped
                                        in blankets:
cappuccino, sweet notes on windshields, gifts,
even the simplest thing a source of intrigue,

like the luna moth he cupped carrying it to class
before letting it go above the heads of students,
soft words, silence after the sexual kisses,
then rumors of ill feelings,
arguments ending with apologies in his office.

He thirsted for serenity he thought he had coming
after years of chemotherapy and prayer,
of doctors at a loss to explain why his wife was still alive
who woke repeatedly dreaming she was already in
                                        her coffin—
of waiting rooms with televisions blaring.

One morning by his Ford Ranger I saw them
and noticed she was the only one
moving her lips. She hurried off, turned back
to emphasize something she wanted to make clear,
her pointed finger shaking him loose from his refusal

to do anything he'd regret and he at last dismissed her
getting into his truck. It was the rage
of having no one else to blame that brought her to
                                        the phone

with words my friend had said against me in dark
harsh judgments, confiding: He has no idea who he is
                                        up against.

I listened. And later heard that she had torched
her mattress on his lawn with gasoline when he was gone,
following with binoculars his flight from house to work
till like the snow that graced the ground for an instant
in late winter, she was gone—a vapor swept away in
                                        April's chill.

Oh they were in love all right and I
in awe of how unjust it was their love was not enough
to soothe the suffering that wanted
so much more, sinister pursuit through neighborhoods,
cryptic scribbling on his door in crimson ink.

And knowing this was so—that this
is the way it is—was like seeing the slender beast
that leaps too soon and loses the gazelle
curving into trees along the river
because of the terrible hunger that it feels.

The Confession

Just south of Birmingham there is a smell
that goes deep when you breathe in,
blown up into the beautiful suburbs
when the wind is westerly; and at evening,
driving north, before the stench
hits you you see the orange tongue of flame
flickering insultingly above the foundry,
above the complicated sprawl of metal
where women and men broil in the heat
that cannot be extinguished by the big fans,
a network of iron and steel that appears
out of nowhere when the interstate lifts
briefly out of the trees. I know
such a bitter description of the world
is typical of someone who would piss
all over himself if he woke
from his dream of personal transcendence
to find himself covered in grit,
shoveling ash filtering down insidiously
through the grates on every level.
Why tell again the old lie of fresh bread
and steamed potatoes and meat
set before the fifty-year-old welder
who has smoked his lungs black
and eaten his heart out and stopped
finally longing for the god of constant attention
to turn away for an instant
so he can scream? I knew a man
like that when I was in my twenties
and not once did he speak of what
he did or refer to the daily pain
of being defeated by the cacophony

impossible to flee, that spits you out
at twilight to a house inherited
from your father, ten miles west
of the odor and clang and indifference
of the beast. On summer evenings
he would sit on his patio with the shade
of the pines reaching across the pond
and drink, flipping a quarter around
in his fingers, the dim silver manipulated
without even thinking. "Phil,"
his wife would say, "Are you coming in?"
and he would smile at me,
sliding lower and lower in his lawn chair
till sleep came and I got up
and went back to my room above his kitchen.

I used to drive past that foundry
thinking of him as he forced himself up
out of his Chevy truck in the lot
at dawn, his work clothes clean,
merging with the long line of other men
soon to be lost inside the din
of Bessemer Steel. And I understood
not everyone is redeemed.
I drove on with my dream,
the one where women cluster and fawn
and the words come quickly
to the testimony of a man imagining what it must
be like to live in every one
of the apartments that swept by.
I drove past the hospital named for a saint,
the cemetery, past the tenement houses
blackened on the hillside,
the food marts, the cathedrals golden and alone. At times,

getting off at the exit
curving up into this desert of stalled cars
and men with plastic garbage bags
bulging with cans, I saw this city
of faces and was amazed,
remembering the pleasure Phil took
stroking the collie he'd gotten from a friend,
the tenderness as he leaned away from the smoke
of the grill on Saturday afternoon
and found in that moment the only hope
there is. Who would want to embellish
the truth that will have to be lived
and not simply imagined,
as final and forthcoming as a semi
seen too late by a driver on the wrong
side of the highway late at night,
sudden death separating the wrist
from the hand as the spirit lingers
then is gone as though it never really existed,
looking back at the significance of everything it did?

I knew a man. And from his kind wife
by the fireplace the weekend after Phil's death
learned he had finally surrendered
with the help of friends,
a fearless self-estimate that left him
sober and changed and impatient for the day
when the refuge of liquor
no longer was necessary and he could witness
the sun coming up above the blast furnaces
as if it were a miracle,
talking late into the evenings
of his dream of being an electrican
and not taking any shit.

Looking at his picture above the mantel I felt the fear
of becoming nameless in this city
where courtesy lay at the center of every prayer,
and drove on in my mind while she told
of how gently he treated
her in the end, past skyscrapers glittering with thousands
of windows and high-rises
and warehouses scrawled with obscenities
in orange letters announcing Armageddon
was already here, until I came to a lake far out in a field
and saw a swan
floating aimlessly dipping its head again and again.

I remember the eloquence of her confession
defining his life by the fireplace,
with nothing better to do than turn a quarter
over endlessly in his hand,
and that she never flinched
admitting Phil was lost from the beginning,
unseen driving off except by Providence
that had its own idea of what was right,
or didn't care, or wasn't there
to care—this last a truth too terrible to consider.
And saying this she began to live.

Pig Iron

The City of Dis begins with the smell of pig iron
making you sick. At night,
    when factories shut down and the neon

above the Bangkok Massage Parlor flashes on,
    you can see the dead
sorting the living into the damned, the redeemable,

    the sure deals shouting commands,
telling us what we loved wasn't enough. You can see
    the flow of people dressed in sweat pants

under the trees that line the polluted lake
    in one of the suburbs
where a woman watches her Pomeranian shit in the
                                public gardens

    with the supreme indifference of an angel
and death follows a child of eight
    who cuts into the woods alongside the highway

because supper is waiting. In the city of mutilation
    God is ground down
and people touch each other tenderly on a screen,

    the surgeon's hand rests delicately
on the forehead of a stranger and an ambulance
                    weaving through traffic
    misses a yellow Cadillac by inches.

    And when the sun glints in the eyes of those
                        coming in

at the mall on One-hundred-Twenty-fifth Street
     the moon appears, and from the inner brilliance

of a kitchen in one of the high rises still lit by the sun
     after twilight, a voice
in the city of sacrifice, the city of pain,

     begins to complain. And you can do nothing
for the suicide sitting on the edge of a bed at Motel 6
     with all of it coming at him,

in the city of revelry where nothing matters
     and even a candle asks too much, in the city
          of grief
where the only relief for the pain is the needle's

     slow insertion. A teenager dressed in red
          leather leans
into the window of a Porsche before getting in,
     and repentance comes with the sun just cresting
          the steeple

at St. Jude's Hospital where the deity nobody needed
     bends beseechingly,
ready to come back and finding it hard to break free.

     Then sleep. And in this sleep a creature
undressing before a mirror
     allows herself to be touched before turning away.

     Sober I have seen men conspire to sell their souls
by giving up everything—the truth appearing for every-
          one to see.
     Taking my way home across the bridge

overlooking the city, with my window lowered,
       I looked at shadowy figures along the ditches,
the whistle announcing another shift, smoke
                     stacks trailing

      their banners indifferently above the misery
of strikers
      too bitter to have mercy, holding their palms out
                         to the fire.

 I was alone and late in understanding
      what it takes to go back over everything,
ransack the past, see if there wasn't something I could

      have done, kind words whispered to
                the adulteress
across the pillow, cupping her hands,
      saying my name so softly it seemed a blessing.

And I can't keep the days from fleeing,
      scent of bonfires and the traveling
of blackbirds across the heavens: a river of minutes,
                hours, seasons.

      Gone is her white nightgown so thin
I could see her thighs,
      gone her leg over mine, the light flicked on

after midnight and the face in the mirror
      at the mercy
of a stare too cruel to be refuted by my mind.

Reading Habits

I always look for the small poem first,
the message tucked inside the stanza
stiffening against
any effort to correct what can't be said
in any other fashion.

Like staring at a sketch
by Michelangelo hinting at something grander,
an inconspicuous countenance
discovered gazing up in his Last Judgment
where even pride is abandoned.

Letter To Elizabeth

I see a satellite across the sky
above a flight of geese. "Coincidence,"
I think, then remember the line
"Leaf returning to its branch—butterfly."
That's Basho. And I reconsider everything again.
But where are you and I in all of this?

In your letter you mention
your courtyard garden where you hunt
"dreaded slugs and snails," amazed
"by the literalness of the picture"—
pecan shells sprouting leaves, sending
"into earth that thin white foot."
I wish I knew what to say to you, Elizabeth.

Imagine you and Basho just after sunrise
standing happily in your garden, laughing,
in his way helping you forget
what you have been through, saying
"Frog on a lily pad. . . plop. . . then Nirvana"—
then with a sidelong look
and smiling: "The way out likewise is the way in."

In the wake of your friend's death
I make my own amends. Of what significance
is He who works in ways mysterious
if we can't sense the imminence of this faint
outline of the full moon moving into our window?
Plant a tomato seedling and watch it grow.
There is resurrection in that.

Easter, 1996

Looking Up At Something

    One night, in Ohio,
  hearing the geese overhead,
    I looked up
and saw what I thought was a flying saucer
  above the town, bright white,
with windows shimmering on the side.
    Ah, it was gone
  before I could point out to my kind
    what flashed
and stopped on a dime. How awful

    to harbor a secret all your life,
  if only half-believed,
    biting your lip
to keep from screaming at everyone around,
  "Do you know what I saw
one night above the clouds?" A disc
    of fire
with the full moon lagging behind.

    Out there,
  where meteors collide and spaceships
    between one universe
and the other abruptly pause, as if
  forbidden to satisfy
 a longing thought reserved for us,
    another God abides
  in love with silence. That night
    I saw
His handiwork and was filled with awe

that such a thing
might be revealed to anyone like us,
intent on seeking
someone who'd look up before withdrawing
into a darkness
too vast to think about. I followed,
coveting that dot
that steered by starlight across the sky

until it found at last
a known ground, letting out souls
that study each other
with mercy that starts in the eyes.
No doubt I should
have shared this with someone wiser,
but I was shy
and too ashamed of whatever it was
to confirm what I suddenly felt about human love.

TWO

This Moment

Alone with the one story, trying to pry it open
with a voice that knows yet will not be controlled,
                                    the light
partially shining on the white page that seems the cause
                                    of your problems
at the moment, handwriting unintelligible in spots,
certain where you hoped to go was wrong and knowing you
                                    will never possess
the image of Uncle Harlan on the couch one summer when
                                    you came home,
alone with the memory of your stopping in the hall
just before he looked up and over his shoulder,
alone with that darkness Rothko adored
in paintings he described as rooms "where all the doors
                                    and windows
are bricked up," that snapshot of Stephanie on the wall
with her arms lifted to that last self-portrait by Van Gogh,
alone with the calendar flipped up in January to June
                                    to show
the inexplicable expression in the face of a woman
                                    reading a letter

————————————————

alone with the sound of the oak outside your window
that speaks of the grief that is merely human.
Alone with the notion of your own mortality
getting up in childhood to steer a glass toward water
and discovering in gossamers of light
your parents driven to one another in the dark,
alone with what you hoped would be your testimony—
alone with the snow falling into tracks leading up to
                                    the door,

with the silence that asks for more than you are willing
to give in this cathedral because you know what's best for
the story
and won't be talked out of it
. . . something indifferent to the truth takes over
and twists
away in a direction that wants to culminate in joy:
a blessing, or holy waste—not witnessed. No.

Holy Waste

"If Galileo had said in verse that the world moved,
  the Inquisition might have left him alone."
                              —Thomas Hardy

First Month

1.

Rilke said something funny about wanting to write
about people after he finished with beasts,
but finding "the highest mystery" of marriage
hard maybe he would skip that and continue beseeching
as he did in *The Duino Elegies*, a pity
but perfectly understandable given his inclination
                                        to withdraw.
This month I see his black-and-white photograph
                              blown up
in a bookstore window and am astonished:
how handsome and intense, how focused,
eyes questioning everything about those
coming in at the mall. He wrote of Rodin: "When others
began to doubt him he no longer doubted himself."

2.

The misanthrope too moody to sit next to,
without his hood and cane, the crone, the ogre,
faces Bruegel would have found a reason to paint,
a murmuring of widows commiserating with each other
in the heat after mid-day Mass. GET RIGHT
WITH GOD OR GET LEFT BEHIND the marquee

reads on my way home.
At a light along Fifteenth Street Father Kelly is alone
in his white Toyota. I am disappointed to see he is
speaking to himself,
then realize he's singing. What a relief.
Why not watch this mystery,
adjusting the rear-view mirror so our eyes don't meet?

3.

It's when I realize I have lost what loveliness
there was that I recall my wife's clear eye for wildflowers.
I wonder what she was thinking
creeping over the lawn on hands and knees,
unaware of what was going on around her.

No wonder so many long for the exquisite jump shot
at the top of the key, the fake to the left
in a sudden drive to the basket
gloriously blue and golden against the west.
And if I had insisted that I was one with the universe,
would she have believed me? Could she?

The sun sheds light through trees when I get out
without my briefcase,
each branch uplifted as I have never seen them.
And I feel again
what wells up in me on evenings when I unfold my chair
and smoke just out of reach of the sprinkler:
The desire to live at the center of the heart of peace.

4.

Lately I have been watching the woman next door
with her dog, splitting my Venetian blinds at dawn
to find them walking in the yard beyond the clothes line
where I hang my quilt hurriedly so I won't have
to talk about how I ended up in this apartment.
Tall and thin, she resembles Stephanie, Louie's wife,
blonde, tolerant, and looking to a life that
                              offered promise
before she began the long fight culminating
at St. Jude's Hospital with everyone in utter silence
                                        outside the door.

There is the portrait of my wife and me
on the wall in full regalia—stiff and dignified.
Easy to romanticize our first meeting and the ease
with which we conversed, she in her checkered dress,
my burgundy tie, neither of us aware
of what the future would like to do
if only we refused to see each other as we are.

5.

I am thankful for this line of fire ants
crossing the walk, bearing the spoils of their hunt
toward some unknown matriarch in languid silence
out in the yard. Nothing to do but thrive.
Her multitudinous servants fawn and feed her
hour after hour food that she devours
out of duty to this metropolis—a monstrous concubine
whose only purpose is to populate.
That makes no sense to my odd mind.

Going in or going out,
these ants don't argue with their way of life.

                   If I could describe my spirit
it would be at rest in shallows reflecting the length
of a heron neither inclined to stay where it is
in shade, nor seeking the flash of a fin.
I should have known better than to even begin.

Second Month

6.

In Grunewald's painting of the crucifixion
Christ looks sick, his feet a mass of muscle, flesh,
his hands at the end of unnaturally long arms
twist and claw. He would like to vomit,
to be done with this. But He loves on.
And nobody knows what I am thinking
watching the slow death of a rhino on TV
stuck in a watering hole in Kenya.
What week is this? What month?

Suddenly the old grief of having thoroughly lost
that other life to someone who understands my love
better than I, rises up seeing couples
embracing on blankets in Sokol Park. They're young
and mild, looking at the overcast
or propped up on one elbow saying nothing at all.
And I wonder how many are married and if this bliss
endures, for surely this seems likely by how they kiss
in full view, getting up
to pull each other in again, delighted by their love.

All at once a kite goes up and everybody stares,
wanting so much for it to remain upright.

7.

I used to watch my wife while she was sleeping
on the couch, Colleen in her green bathrobe
with a serene expression she rarely
had in her waking life, rolled over on her side.
Opening her eyes at times, looking around
and finding nothing wrong, she'd withdraw
once more to whatever offered so much comfort
away from this house. And I remember the night
she grasped my hand after Stephanie's death and told me
I had to be proud of what I'd done
and I told her she was the only woman
I would ever love. Now she's gone
with the taste of that declaration on my tongue.

8.

An anecdote about Fydor Dostoyevsky
after he had been married no more
than a year: Coming into his study
where his wife sat scribbling he saw her slip
something into her shawl,
an attempt on her part to make him jealous
because she assumed this was a sign of love. Half-mad,
stricken with epilepsy throughout his life,
this was enough to drive him over the edge
till she was able to explain what she had done.

Or have I failed to remember this correctly
because I have come to believe
love is not possible without tremendous suffering? In
                                                his diary
Dostoyevsky wrote (What must she have been thinking
to conceive such a trick
on this prisoner of the labyrinth of the mind?):
"Writing is like walking around yourself and watching."

9.

Don't forget the little white schoolhouse just off
                                highway 34
to Howes, South Dakota. Don't forget the paired swings,
that teeter-totter, the rusted water pump by the gravel path,
the oil drum with the grate where trash was incinerated.
Don't forget the bright red sign on the front door saying
THIS IS A TOBACCO FREE WORK PLACE and the sun
blazing beyond the shadow of the hillside. And don't forget
that hawk you saw slowly riding the wind on the other side
of the highway with the sun passing behind a small cloud
off to the right. Don't forget it flooded the plains with light.

10.

Was it Van Gogh who wrote that the only painters
capable of capturing Christ's face were Delacroix
and Rembrandt? What of Zuburan's
soft flesh and downturned eyes against a background
that seems to isolate Him further?

                                    And I remember Goya
letting Christ out of his mind with his revisions of Toledo
In A Thunderstorm, the donors in the foreground
the first to go with a black sky massing
I recognized one summer coming home.
Imagine no identity. No life after death.
The husband who wants out of a marriage
because his wife just lies there.
Imagine not remembering who you are.

This is a journey, a sort of quest if you will, so hurry up
but hurrying the heart forgets
or sees so little it might as well have refrained
from the climb. Take your foot off the pedal. Come to
                                                    a stop.

11.

The glass doors part, the receptionist grins,
her auburn hair drawn back by a hand
studded with rings. "Have you been here recently?"
I take a seat beside a child asleep
and page through *Newsweek's* photographs of people
murdered in a week: Linda. Daryl. Diane.

Then the clean fields and glittering courts
of *Sports Illustrated*, fervent letters from lonely fans:
Sioux Falls. Denver. Spokane. In my briefcase
I find a poem by Auden written in my hand,
which I memorize beginning at the end.
His "dreadful martyrdom."

The man with stomach cramps looks up
at the receptionist and winces, "I don't need this shit."
Where is my wife? Who will help me with this?

12.

I show the mole to the doctor behind my back after
                                        he's coaxed
out of me the confession "I'm upset,"
my shirt over my head while he touches that
                                        tropical island
of malevolence with his thumb,
saying "It's kind of charcoal colored
around the edge—but I don't think it's cancer."
Then he leans back on the counter
crossing his arms. "You've got duodenitis and
we'll treat it as such. Take your medicine. Don't smoke."

Along the garden path a bumble bee investigates,
end up, the mind of an iris. I love that.

13.

Cop cars and ambulances parked outside Classic's Lounge
and, across the avenue,
men in black jackets walking around with coffee:
A moment of high drama driving to my office.
I circle the neighborhood, pause,
roll my window down when I see a sharpshooter
behind a pile of garbage waiting for the opportunity
                                        to fire.
Someone is being held hostage inside the bar

and neighbors have come out to fantasize from driveways
what it must be like with nothing but survival or suicide
on your mind, their lust for life revived
watching in dreadful silence by the highway.

That night on the news I see myself in my car,
elbow out the window, and am disgusted. So this
is what I have come to, and Jesus, and I am not invisible
                                                    at all.

14.

I have been trying to find a book on meadows
like those I looked at in my childhood,
whole chapters describing the metamorphosis
of winter into fall. In my mind's eye
I see the lives of beetle and mice
in black and white in the corner, stages of the moth,
the red-winged blackbird along the fringe
of a pond. I see that meadow as if it really exists,
with wind that hungers up the hillside,
then the silhouette of a man getting out
of his truck that he's left running by the highway.

And when it's dusk the butterflies diminish,
returning to their roosts among the passionflowers
till sunlight touches the warm weeds again
and wings are open fully.

I would like to spend one year intently watching.
Then I would not be afraid of what I have become.

Third Month

15.

"When you are at loose ends get out the only thing you
                                              love
more than yourself," my father said, meaning the
                        clarinet, "and have at it,"
advice that seemed wildly off the mark
though now I understand enough to drive to a field
spreading into a valley. There, where nothing matters,
certain I am being listened to
by something that feels nothing but affection,
I begin, "Our Father, Who art in heaven. . ."
then am distracted by a yellow jacket
that won't relent, wheeling around my head.

When I was ten a friend explained the universe
had no end, expanding into what
did not exist. Should I have looked this up
to see if what I thought was not correct,
every star the product of a deity
driven to perplex a child as gullible as this?
How might my father have responded
if this dilemma had presented itself to him?
With prayer? With the clarinet?

16.

All these fallen and falling leaves and I have never
witnessed the detachment of a single leaf
from its branch, a lesson in humility looking out
the window with my cat at mockingbirds on the lawn.

Gone, another flock alights and flutters out of sight,
reappearing as a single cardinal that stares up
with this evening's light. The cat is enamored
of the cardinal and could listen all night long
if such an aria were possible from dusk to dawn.
But darkness takes the cardinal away. Another day?
I feel safe when it's just dark enough not
to be seen, in profile by the window craning as if to hear
a silent consciousness calling for prayer,
with the moon on the verge of becoming less than itself.

17.

The ballet of those two mayflies in the window
recalls for me those "paired butterflies" in a poem
I found years ago by someone hopeless and alone
in a hospital on the coast, St. Elizabeth's,
a symbol that lives for me and reinforces the theme
of human thirst because it is not a prerequisite to art.
All desire to influence what occurs is lost
when singleness of voice excludes the poet
who will lose his way in the war. Once
I asked Stephanie to recite "The River-Merchant's Wife:
A Letter" and am still haunted by how beautifully
it was performed, the melancholy lover looking out
across the river with such hope
of her coming out to greet the one she loved "As far as
                                        Cho-fu-Sa."

18.

This is the way it is. No one can halt
the ascent of the sun or that entourage of mourners
following a cop up Skyland Boulevard
flashing blue lights until the last car passes
and he curves off. He is certain of his life,
believing wrong from right, and hasn't time
for those who intimate it might be otherwise.

At 8:05 behind the register at Buddy's
the clerk in her blue uniform lets me have my coffee,
sending me off with a voice so gentle I am almost tempted
to turn around. This is the dilemma
I am wrestling with
except on nights when next to the window I recall
my own advice. And I must find some solace in this life.

19.

   What is vision? Truly I do not know
what shows itself a mirror of the soul
   until I move through Keats' poem to autumn
and see that he's not there at all,
   is everywhere, nothing, no one,
surrounded by and surrounding all that flows,
   finished with the argument that drives
the poem and acknowledging the immeasurable calm
   and struggling to behold
this season "sitting careless on a granary floor."

I know the mind that opens is no mind at all
   "among the river sallows."

Those little solar systems of gnats that mourn
  in sudden marriage of one to the other
describe the soul. See how he yearns.
  See how he turns from the close
of summer and revives the metaphor for us all.

20.

The interstate for a minute rises above the city
and I see, in mindless flight, the sun. What
in the world is happening to me?

Imagine St. Francis walking the shoulder bent under
the weight of aluminum cans. He checks
the dumpsters, gets in, looks up at the limousine
                              backing out
behind the Holiday Inn.

At twilight a butterfly has undertaken to cross
the street and is successful,
though its flight is into the wind. I park, get out,
a silence at St. John's Church with a prayer for
                              Sylvia Plath
whom I imagine with her head in the oven,
no longer scared, alone with herself at last.

I have imagined what must love suffering
so much it would do anything to keep
it alive, sung with such force
silence seemed the only response for us all,
grinning idiotically at those I can't avoid
in doorways and at corners,
barely willing even to open my mouth.

Remember Goya's scenes of revelry?
Any regrets?

I wish I had held the hand of Emily Dickinson.

21.

She was a light-colored moth
blown into the room through one of the many
                              dark windows.
With the wasp and fly
she kept counsel, seeking (who knows why)
every lamp shade, every flame.
Fresh from the world,
around and around she whirled, tormented by the enigma
of a window pane.

She found peace in a white dress.
She found terror in senseless flight.

That night, window to window she drifted,
compliant, keeping her faith,
pattering out her life upon a sill
where she was found by someone who released her into
                                        the night
toward whatever light.

22.

Something I can't see is beginning to pay
close attention to me. It bends

in the darkness and measures the depth when I try to sleep.
There are moments when I can reach out and almost feel it.

23.

I wanted the long fields of autumn, the fragrance of clover,
the maple and the oak, a lake, a single hawk.
I wanted a graveyard smaller than a garden,
a weather-vane pointing perpetually northward,
wanted the bridal gown of snow and ghoul of smoke
withering above the chimney in December.
I wanted the innocence of it all.

THREE

Directions

Go back to the Passion
where a man is whipped and cursed through the streets,
a crossbeam cutting all down his shoulder.
Go into the howling to get a better look
at what it means to be singled out for good reason,
shoved forward, hoping for a glimpse of the one who trips
clinging to the rough wood.

Go back with your hands
behind your back and somebody holding your cheeks
so you can't turn away from the corpses gathered
by a bulldozer into an enormous grave where a child
is flung above them all with remarkable ease.

Go to the black oven
in the brick wall where burnt flesh testifies
to the terrible concession that in the light of day
you won't relinquish, to the one who willed this—
go back to this.

And when the beautiful hymns
are sung during Mass, summon the image of Auschwitz
from above after a thunderstorm,
children in white livery, men who all look the same.
After you have stared into evil
you can return to the purity again and not be mistaken.

Litany

When Thomas Hardy let himself be dragged

to a local tavern by his companions
(who felt he was not having

fun),
he looked out a window for hours

at a cemetery while they roared with laughter,
prodding him to join in.

Let this simple blessing remember him.

And when everyone cried out
at Descartes to come forth and be merry with wine,

women and song,
he packed all he had into a carriage

and escaped to the country,
temporarily at peace
in a cottage surrounded by wild chrysanthemums.

And when Franz Kafka read *The Metamorphosis*
to his friends

they thought the story was hilarious.
And he fled back to his desk
where nothing could appease his hunger.

And when Boris Pasternak got a call
one night from Stalin

who wanted to know

    why Pasternak was going out of his way to defend
        Osip Mandlestam

    he invited Stalin to have a talk

      about life and death,
whereupon Stalin abruptly hung up.

      And when, dressed up
to look like one of the more famous painters

    of the day, one of Henri Rousseau's
  close friends
knocked on his door to say he had come

      because one great painter ought to pay homage
to another,
            Rousseau with a smile responded
"I have been waiting for you a long while."

*

To write the story of love and death

      one long continuous thread
  enters the flesh
          and separates the minstrel
  from the rest, the Dean, the Doctor of Internal Medicine,
the Receptionist. I lift my pen.

What it means to be among the living and the dead.

The Leopard

The living have many faces; the dead, one.

When the leopard comes down out of the forest
everyone is awed. It comes down

without a sound through the long grass of the savannah
bypassing the herds of Thompsin's gazelle

in the glow of the moon on a cloudless night
beginning to glide toward lights this side

of the river, a swiftness
startling a bird straight up. We hear the cry

of the hyena again, maniacally happy over the death
of a wildebeest dragged down from behind

as the leopard slows then comes to rest
across the road from a Somali woman and child,

then later drags that child up into the trees
to keep it from being devoured by the lions.

There, where screams can be identified
by the hyena at night, the leopard crouches

at the base of a tree before it leaps
lost in leaves concealing everything.

At dawn the leopard licks its paws
no longer hungry for the heart of a child

disemboweled alongside a limb in early fall
where the eclipse of the moon shocks

even the strongest warrior
and the leopard sees us for who we really are.

The Anaconda

The man with the anaconda around his neck
seems proud, letting it coil and slide

across his outstretched arm and cupping
the throat as gently as a sparrow.

He has arrived
to flaunt his fearless love at noon

to traffic on the highway,
wrapped up in this tough-minded muscle that shares

his days in a cage of glass demanding all,
flickering his tongue, the habitual

tic of a thief alone in the night,
thick and glistening, threading its length

gently up around his shoulders now
and weaving the delicate wedge-head in the air.

The anaconda does not seem to care
that it will be carried out to be admired

on Greensboro Avenue with its master
smirking at those who linger along the highway,

as if he alone possessed
the courage to confront this gliding dream

embracing everything. The anaconda feels
but begins to hunger for something other

than what it feels, flashing
between the master's spreading feet,

projecting its sexual head
like a wild idea, looking behind and around,

like a hand thrown up by a child,
nude, with nothing human on its mind.

And when the master grows tired
of presenting this labyrinth of flesh to the crowd,

folding and unfolding above the ground,
too feverish to receive his several kisses

offered to demonstrate his love,
he unwinds the willing creature with difficulty,

pouring it into the cage beside his bed
with patience won from things done right,

as if the anaconda were the embodiment of knowledge,
or consciousness wedded to consciousness

in a moment of clarity, hidden in stillness:
vainglorious, passionate, precise.

Shadows

In photographs of the frozen dead
near Stalingrad, there is a gesture,
the hands and feet outstretched
as if to express what it is like to be impaled
by a bayonet

yet remain this side
of death. "Who do you love?
Who do you desire more than anyone else?"

And on the streets if you look closely
you can see shadows cast by the gutted storefronts
where somebody has stumbled over the corpse
of a cart-horse

burned black in the aftermath,
shadows that shrink back,
vanish,
lengthen over the rubble in the other direction

till they are swallowed up
and the moon
clears the only tree for miles around
with this perpetual question: "Who did you die for?
Who will you sacrifice?"

And in the story of Christ
before he capitulates there is this instant
when he regrets everything,
as if he hadn't the heart for this, absolute agony

like the screaming hinge of a door,
stopping everyone in a circle of whirling grit,
including the initiate
whose has taken her place beside the high priests
in their ceremonial hats

and the soldiers who are supposed to know
what they are doing. Mary
is helped to her feet,
Christ lifted almost gingerly, wrapped in white linen

with a thin strip around his neck,
enabling anyone
to flick back the head covering in answer
to the question "Who is this?"

Separated, at last,
from those who would let you suffer
another death,
your faith questioned by your lessors,
did you ever imagine the furnaces of Buchenwald

might come to pass
walking out with the rain beginning to fall
all over Galilee, your silence broken
and the voice of your rough companion calling after?

Sister, Sister

What's done is done, my love
a syllable of blood and thirst and hunger—

but because I am suddenly afraid for you,
your right hand steering downward into the light,
knowing the work you do, knowing how you despise it,
because of the judgment of your forefinger,
the underside lifted lingeringly toward the one leaning back
                                                on her heels
who wishes to listen,
because you are so far gone in the world of men,
I walk out past the houses where the desert begins.

Somewhere out there in uneasy sleep
the serpent dreams. The wind shrieks. The orange
                              blossom of the cactus
closes. And a hooded nomad riding the silhouette
of a camel into Bethany
rocks back and forth in purple garments woven out of silk.

God watches. The god of longing.
Of level plains and sickle moons above a glittering city.

Somewhere out there an artisan in his eighties
turns over the pages of an ancient text,
finds the noun "spine," the noun "parchment,"
licks his finger, goes on reading.
Somewhere out there a mosque fills the sky with screams,
words come haltingly to the paralytic
whispering to the night nurse in the infirmary with her
                              back to the window,

to the stone-cutter drunk on vinegar again
straining to elaborate on the immorality of women.
In another minute, he will step out
and be struck by a busload of tourists from Nagasaki.

Because you have imagined the massaging of oil
over the splayed bones and bitterly disagreed with this,
worked and served, argued your own ache,
because nothing can be done,
because the scheme of cause and effect is a mystery
even as you lean and speak,
hands callused from years in the kitchen,
because you are sick of it and seek to intervene,

somewhere out there, gently now, what the master
                                        has completed
begins to sing. And the face in the basin,
the face of the god you wanted,
takes issue with what must be re-conceived,
must be done differently. And when the world has turned
to constitute a day remember everything you hated
as one who has been changed.
Sister, sister. Leaf to lost leaf.
Straighten your finger. Let it rest on me.

(Tintoretto, "Christ in The House of Mary and Martha")

Afternoon Nap

And the lotus flower opens on the water
as if the Master thought it into blossom.

Pausing Between One Page And Another In A Novel By Wallace Stegner

It's then I think of the compass,
rusted, underfoot when I stepped to the edge

of the pond that summer in strange childhood,
dug up from matted grass and looked at

in my hands, the needle pointing perpetually northward,
and lost, coming down through shale

with the last of the sun
spreading everywhere over the meadow, a prize

backtracked for at twilight,
never found. It's out there, wedged between boulders

with the deep dream of winter run-off flowing over

it in spring
that a child couldn't find even if he took the simple path

circling back through cottonwoods,
went down on his knees for, hunted for years.

It's out there. Somewhere.
And I have begun to understand why I must love it.

*

Listen, after the last splash of lightning
for thunder
which does not come as a crack but somebody
mumbling uncontrollably

on the horizon, cross the backyard
in lamplight of the kitchen window.

A whippoorwill begins
from the center of all darkness to sing.

You've got it in your head to seek again,

grasp that cold metal
in your grown palm before the last truth
        veiled by the cry of the night heron rising at dusk

        claims you, lays you out,
unraveling tongues of fire in and around

        your body in a coffin that goes nowhere,
a remnant, that speaks with the click click

        of branches crusted with ice
in mid winter, makes you tireless

                to say: My childhood was a huge tree
        uprooted in a thunderstorm

        that lay across the roof of the house for days.

My childhood was flight from door to door
behind the love chest embroidered with rubies

and darkened brass

and I tell lies as if I had tried them out
        a hundred times.

I was slender and never went out alone
without the compass I found in a field of clover.

*

Needle. I can believe in that word,
as kindness come to the father of leaves like a daughter,

learned, lived with
nightlong in sickness with the sweet ghost

of scarlet fever,
twisting in the sheets my mother snapped

in the twilight, then folded
like a shroud for one of the many dead

showing the way,
that craving for inexplicable glitter

gone into the mind's
absolute blackness, needle that does nothing,
serves no purpose,
is resurrected in memory again and again.

Around the compass
trembling in no direction, the wilderness spins.

*

Not wildfire crackling
over the prairie, not hunger, mercy, love.

Not the nightwash of wind

coming into the pin oak turned white in moonlight.

        Not what it means to let go
of godforsakenness
    of preternatural darkness absolutely without flaw,

     the compass uncovered as if it knew
the truth
     along the ridges of goldenrod and laurel.

        How something so small
could haunt you, hear you out
     in this dawn-hour of your awakening

     in a house
where the chrysanthemum whispers and needs,
   isn't clear.
             The light not on,
      stillness startling at first, you begin to feel

  everything breathing around you.

       And for an instant
from the deep center all things have in common

     you know that cry, the hum of metal
in the mind. It is the first morning

    of the world,
and the compass is still and utterly giving itself.

From One Who Knew Him Intimately
—Primo Levi (1919-1987)

Everything he saw. Everything he felt.
Sleep. It would come. It would be cleansing.
The faces of the damned are the faces of the living.
Lightly let the violin begin,
the trembling flute *farfalla in tempesta*.
Let the shadow of the withering one
be still, for the confessional, for the canticle,
anguished out of the bones of the cramped hand.

The bones know. What calls to us
calls blissfully. Oyster. Snail.
But if you made your bed in hell
would they pursue you even there?
Here is the word and what it stood for,
clear nights and the whole world listening.
You will know the end. What the bones know.
And there is pity. And there is long forgiving.

Let the single string continue, the flute
half lifted, followed by mute misery,
the singleness of history—every name.
The graciousness of every question.
There is the unbearable blessing.
There is hatred in the cup of cool broth.
The need for sleep. The need for expiation.
What this man wrote about was beauty.

The Kiss

"Come," she said, and looked at the beam
to indicate the silence
   in the room overhead, her father fast asleep

    on the sofa, in a tee-shirt

 shoes off, socks on
    She drew me into the darkness of the cellar

    closing one door, then the other
shutting out the sky

   that showed a sickle moon
     riding the Methodist spire above the town

     And the smell of her was everywhere
like a narcissus in the night

   and all that I was was gone
into that gloom of crates and jars,
   clutching her naked underarm to keep from falling

   "Careful," she said and fumbled
for the banister with a hand
    that shone by the light of a single bulb

    beneath the stair,
stark fingers ringed and slender, sliding her palm

   I saw the ancient machinery in a corner
     wrapped in a cloud of exhausted cobwebs
   the little engine painstakingly taken apart

I saw my shadow

      vast on the wall   and heard
"I'm over here" from the one in darkness,
     still fully dressed, hair down,
  a blanket across the mattress

She was beckoning by opening both arms

    And I let her pull me down
beneath her father's house

    loosening her belt, her bra
by reaching around and flinging it
    a flash in the night   The kiss

    so long in coming is what I recall,
first breath of morning
    up from the pond, scented with wet autumn

          I kissed everything I saw,
    the nape of her neck after sweeping
her hair aside, her taut thigh

    And the Ah of her was all
      that I wanted and thundering of the heart

in this dungeon below the dark,
    while she stopped to listen—gripping my thighs—
     for what she thought
was her father   And night came flying

     like wind wound wildly round
    the cypress in silhouette

beside the barn, and I was inside and out

    of myself with nothing on
        and Kathleen supple in my arms

      when I rolled over looking up
    in wonder at the sight

    of someone far more beautiful for having drawn
                        me down
by reaching out her hand and saying "Come."

Canticle For The Conclusion Of Spring

There are fields, pastures, prairies. There are
deserts too. This blue field in mist
where one tree looms
as if it had the understanding of a thousand years
knows what it knows: there is truth in words.

In June, the clover flourishes. It covers
what remains of a long season gone to ruin.
And the wasp burrows
inside the simple sanctuary of an iris.
Someone you love has pointed this out to you.

At dawn the field is the morning,
at dusk, the evening prayer, and everywhere
as on a monumental table set for two
one star searches.
No moon ministers to this immeasurable view.

It was not bitterness that led you
away from what endures. Let the desert
of the heart have what it wanted from the world.
You were not equal to that argument
of wind and dunes. You simply persevered.

Now the language of the hour spurns
that journey begun in earnest
which goes everywhere and, going everywhere, stays
where it is. Nothing could be more curious.
You should have protected yourself from the first.

Original Pleasure

Summer understands what summer loves,
the path to the house around a grove of hackberries
standing with their hands up in the air,
an anecdote about one
flamboyant flower bestowing orange petals
on the asphalt—dew on window sills.

The drunken hum of bees above a blossom
pleases, as does a dark barn,
bats at twilight flashing below the moon,
wind in a blue and wandering way
diminishing around midnight and two women, nude,

nearing the wide lake of their dreams
where they darken with the water
lukewarm in June. A chrysalis
comes first, soldered to the underarm
of a birch, in summer's love of what
is overlooked by eyes like mine, mosquitoes

confessing their secrecies in malicious prayer,
the toad alone below the tulip
smart as a Buddha. Sandra,
I like the way you arrived at a pool
in your poem, moving as summer moves.

To understand what love is
is to be ravished by language, by August
already gone, withdrawn from under the touch
of one who loves too much
each leaf and labors daily to regain
original pleasure—the greenest hue.

Last Will And Testament

Bequeath. You can have it all
except for the smell of snow before it falls
                    in South Dakota,
that first blizzard in late October coming home
from Washington Elementary thinking how unusual
this feeling evoked by snow
with no one to explain this is the beginning
of the soul. You can have it all:

the knowledge of Immanuel Kant walking
precisely the same time every night,
Gaugin's trying to get away from Vincent Van Gogh,
the hit to right that brought Bobby Elwanger home,
the joy of the illustrator on his deathbed in 1827
drawing one more portrait of his wife.

But not the snow. Let that remain with me.
The drift of it when the world is windless
covering first the yards, then streets, then trees,
and everyone embarrassed by how ecstatic
they feel. I used to open my palm

to see if what they said was true,
each flake created differently as a lesson
on the variety of humans, not anything
close to a doppleganger to refute the ruthlessness
what we do we do. Who would have thought

the one I loved would love me in return,
that prayer would become appeal
for nothingness I couldn't touch at St. John's Church?
Take the prairie on fire in June, the pleasure

in getting up to piss after midnight
with the full moon streaming through the window. No

voices either. Nothing of the shrieks,
the lamentations, the shouts at the door,
my wife of ten years clasping hands and asking
if there was anything at all that she could do.
Let that go. Let that be transformed.

Snow and a voice. Snow and a sigh.
The sigh of awe. The sigh of the catastrophe avoided.
Sleep. And the scent of snow
that summons surrender this last morning in August
of something that never belonged to me at all.

In The Light Of My Lamp

You are a spider and yet
I count your legs to only seven,
daddy long-leg marching across the blank
page of my typewriter then over
the portable phone, all legs
with a dot for a body like a dilapidated ladder
unfolded—no one would think of Coole
and that missing swan
but the one who looks at you this Sunday,
speechless Muse, Minerva,
suddenly pausing I know not why
for the longest time
beside my elbow in the twilight of my house.

Here. You have nothing
but the enigma of our being
to live with for a minute,
the page you make nothing of
as if sentences were better unsaid,
speech unreceived. What dank
corner have you chosen
to be alone, only to reappear
years later to someone else
when I am long since gone? Golden
in the light of my lamp and reluctant
for reasons I can't imagine
to walk off with great strides,
I'd like to give you this
and know that you existed,
puzzled over, one leg gone,
with grace going up and over and out.

AEE-5141